AF575083

An Eye on Spiders

Jumping Spiders

by Jenna Lee Gleisner

Bullfrog Books

Ideas for Parents and Teachers

Bullfrog Books let children practice reading informational text at the earliest reading levels. Repetition, familiar words, and photo labels support early readers.

Before Reading

- Discuss the cover photo. What does it tell them?
- Look at the picture glossary together. Read and discuss the words.

Read the Book

- "Walk" through the book and look at the photos. Let the child ask questions. Point out the photo labels.
- Read the book to the child, or have him or her read independently.

After Reading

- Prompt the child to think more. Ask: Have you ever seen a jumping spider? What more would you like to learn about them?

Bullfrog Books are published by Jump!
5357 Penn Avenue South
Minneapolis, MN 55419
www.jumplibrary.com

Library of Congress Cataloging-in-Publication Data

Names: Gleisner, Jenna Lee, author.
Title: Jumping spiders / by Jenna Lee Gleisner.
Description: Minneapolis, MN : Jump!, Inc., [2018]
Series: An eye on spiders | Includes index.
Audience: Ages 5–8. | Audience: K to grade 3.
Identifiers: LCCN 2017039994 (print)
LCCN 2017046648 (ebook)
ISBN 9781624967931 (ebook)
ISBN 9781624967924 (hardcover : alk. paper)
Subjects: LCSH: Jumping spiders—Juvenile literature.
Spiders—Juvenile literature.
Classification: LCC QL458.42.S24 (ebook)
LCC QL458.42.S24 G54 2018 (print) | DDC 595.4/4—dc23
LC record available at https://lccn.loc.gov/2017039994

Editor: Kristine Spanier
Book Designer: Molly Ballanger

Photo Credits: Shark_749/Shutterstock, cover; Zety Akhzar/Shutterstock, 1; D. Kucharski K. Kucharska/Shutterstock, 3; SANDIREN/Shutterstock, 4; David West/Dreamstime, 5; Kim Taylor/Nature Picture Library/Getty, 6–7, 20–21, 23tr, 23mr; YoONSpY/Shutterstock, 8–9; Brad Sharp/age fotostock, 10, 23ml; Phisit Phochiangrak/Dreamstime, 11; Agustin Esmoris/Minden Pictures/Superstock, 12–13; Cornel Constantin/Shutterstock, 14–15; Barcroft Media/Getty, 16; John Serrao/Science Source, 17, 23tl; Simon Shim/Shutterstock, 18–19, 23bl; Drakuliren/Shutterstock, 20; KangGod/Shutterstock, 22; magnetix/Shutterstock, 23br; blewulis/iStock, 24.

Printed in the United States of America at Corporate Graphics in North Mankato, Minnesota.

Table of Contents

Pouncing on Prey

A jumping spider hides.
It watches.

It jumps!

It pounces on its prey.

These spiders do not need webs.

They can jump far.

Jumping spiders are small.
They move fast!
They can move sideways.

Some are tan.
Others are black.
They have markings.

This one is green!

They like sunlight.

Why?

It helps them see better.

See its eyes?
It has eight!

eyes

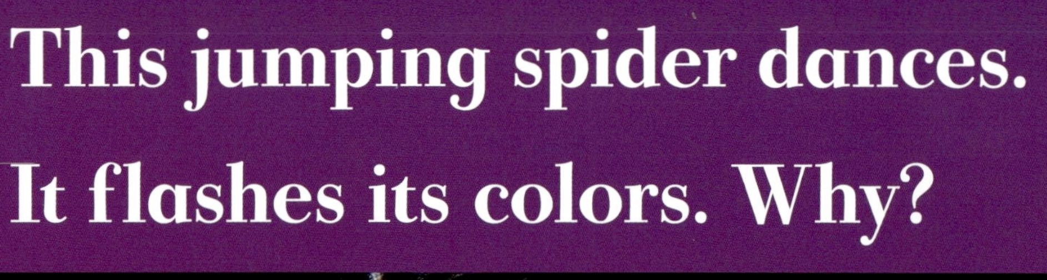

This jumping spider dances. It flashes its colors. Why?

It wants attention.
Does the female notice?

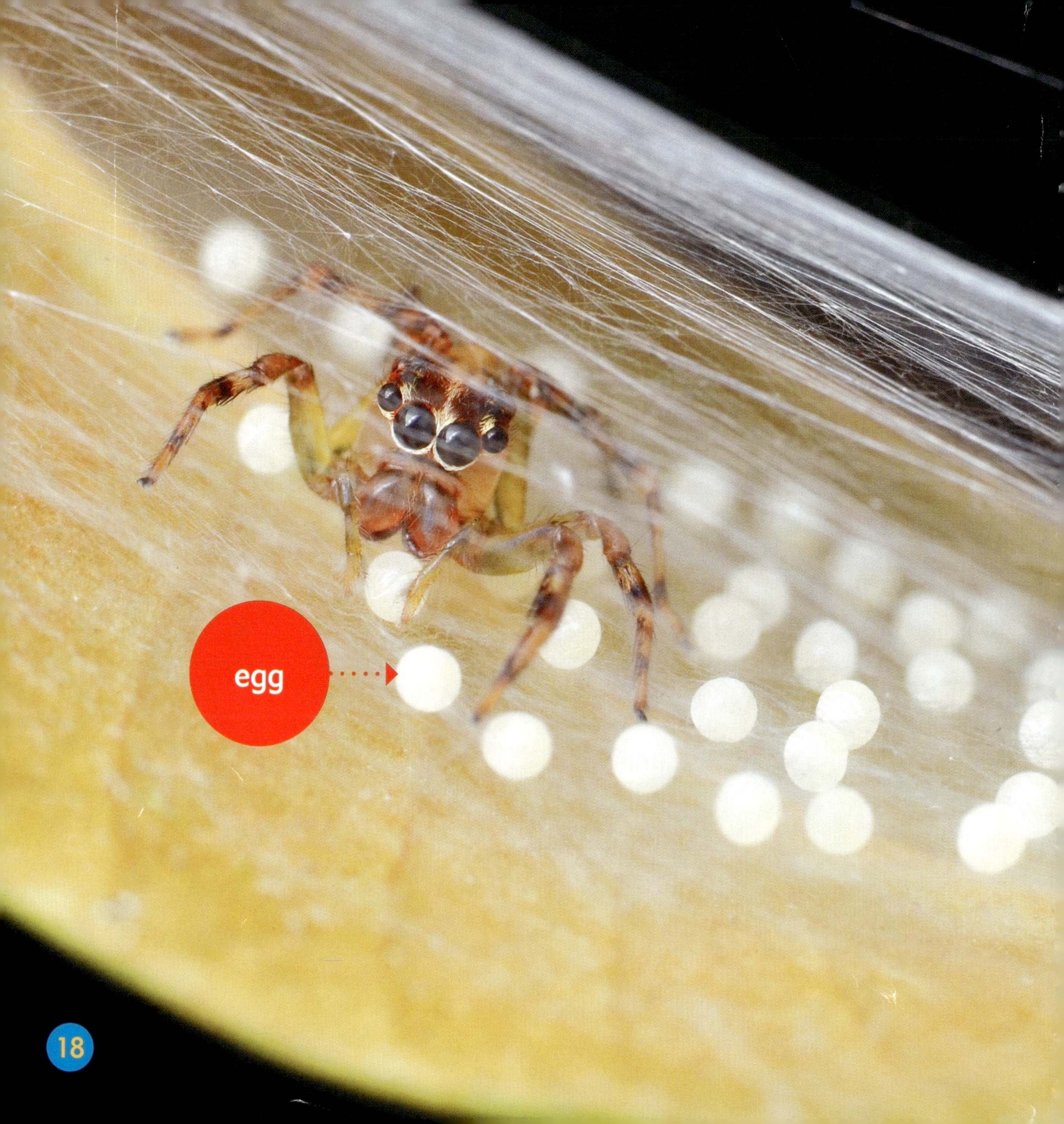
egg

Jumping spiders make silk.

Why?

To keep their eggs safe.

Oh, no!

A hungry bird!

The spider jumps
to safety.

Where in the World?

There are many kinds of jumping spiders. They prefer warm, tropical places. But they can live anywhere in the world except for Antarctica.

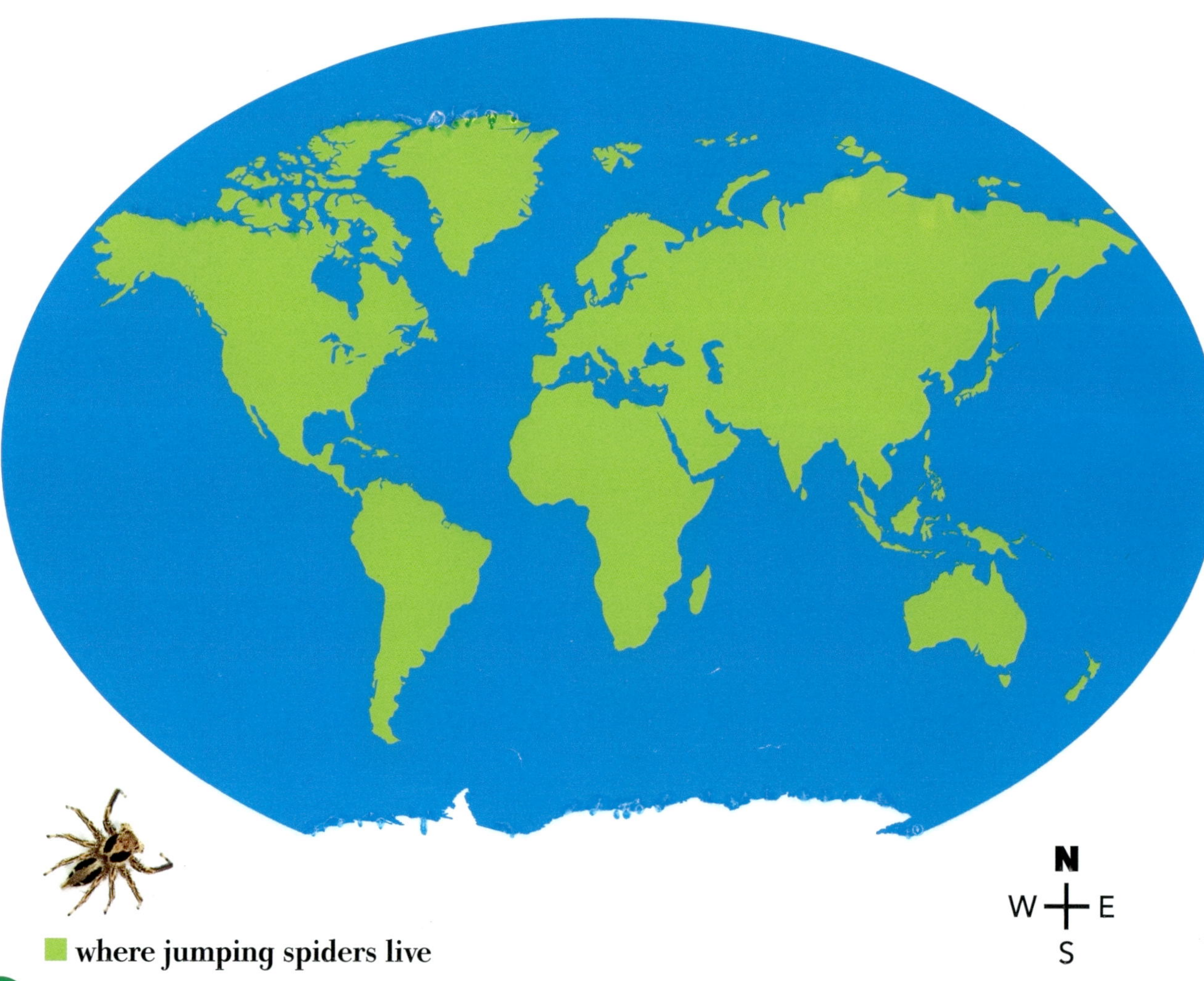

where jumping spiders live

Picture Glossary

attention
Concentration on one thing.

prey
An animal that is hunted by another animal for food.

markings
Spots or patterns.

silk
Fine fibers spiders make to build webs or nests.

pounces
Jumps and grabs something suddenly.

webs
Thin nets spiders make with silk to catch prey.

Index

To Learn More

Learning more is as easy as 1, 2, 3.

1) Go to www.factsurfer.com

2) Enter "jumpingspiders" into the search box.

3) Click the "Surf" button to see a list of websites.

With factsurfer.com, finding more information is just a click away.